Comprehens

INFERENCE

LEVEL B

Executive Editor: Diane Sharpe
Project Editor: Melinda Veatch
Design Coordinator: Sharon Golden
Project Design: Howard Adkins Communications
Cover Illustration: Rhonda Childress
Photographs: ©Tony Freeman / PhotoEdit

ISBN 0-8114-7835-1

4 5 6 7 8 9 0 VP 96

Making an inference means making a guess. You can make this guess by putting together what you know and what you read or see. You will make inferences about the stories in this book.

You make inferences all the time. Look at the picture. How do you feel when you win a game? Who do you think is winning this game? What helped you make this inference?

What Is an Inference?

An inference is a guess you make after thinking about what you already know. For example, a friend invites you to a party. From what you know about parties, you might infer that there will be games, gifts, food, and drinks.

An author does not write every detail in a story. If every detail were told, stories would be long and boring. And the main point would be lost. Suppose you read, "Pat went to the grocery store." The writer would not have to tell you what a grocery store is. The writer expects you to know that it is a place where people buy food. When you hear the words "grocery store," you may think of long rows of shelves with canned foods. Or you may think of cases filled with cheese and milk. By filling in these missing details, you could infer that Pat went to the store to buy food. The writer expects you to infer the missing details from what you know.

Try It!

Read this story about Sam. Think about the facts in the story.

Sam's Morning

Sam walked down the hall at school. He pushed back his straight, red hair with one hand. He hadn't combed it. He rubbed his eyes with a fist. He hadn't washed his face. His shirt was wrinkled. One shoelace was untied. It dragged along the floor as he walked.

How to Make an Inference

Look at the story about Sam again. Look at the facts in the story. They will help you make an inference about Sam. Write the facts on the lines. The first one has been done for you.

Fact 1: Sam had forgotten to comb his hair.

Fact 2: He hadn't ______________________.

Fact 3: His shirt ______________________.

Fact 4: One shoelace ______________________.

Now try to make an inference about Sam. Do you think Sam cares about how he looks?

Inference: Sam ______________________.

- Look at all the facts in the story. Sam hadn't combed his hair. He hadn't washed his face. His shirt was wrinkled. One shoelace was not tied.
- Now go beyond what you've read. What can you guess about Sam? Your inference will come from what you read and what you already know. Did you guess that Sam doesn't care about how he looks? You can infer that because Sam hadn't combed his hair or washed his face. Also, his shirt was wrinkled, and his shoelace was not tied.

Practice Making Inferences

After you read each story, you will answer a question. The question asks you to make an inference about the story.

Read the stories on this page. Answer the questions. The first one has been done for you.

There was a knock at the front door. When June opened the door, she was surprised. Standing there was her friend Mark. He had come to bring her flowers.

__C__ **1.** Which of these sentences is probably true?

A. Mark brought candy for June.
B. June knew that Mark was coming.
C. Mark wanted to do something nice for June.

The correct answer is C. The story says that June was surprised when Mark brought her flowers. From what you read and what you know, you can infer that Mark wanted to do something nice for June.

Grace hurried home from school to check her mailbox. Inside was a letter addressed to her. She tore open the envelope. She quickly read the letter. "Oh! I can't wait!" said Grace. "Sue will be here next week!"

_____ **2.** Which of these sentences is probably true?

A. Grace was happy that Sue was coming.
B. Grace didn't want Sue to visit.
C. Grace was sad that Sue had written.

To check your answer, turn to page 62.

How to Use This Book

Read the stories in this book. Answer the question after each story.

You can check your own answers. If you wish, tear out pages 59 through 62. Find the unit you want to check. Fold the answer page on the dotted line to show the correct unit. Line up the answer page with the answers you wrote. Write the number of correct answers in the score box at the top of the page.

You can have fun with inferences. Turn to pages 56 through 58, and work through "Think and Apply."

Remember

Each question has one answer. Sometimes you may think two of the answers are correct. If that happens, read the story again. Be sure to choose the best answer.

Hints for Better Reading

- Read the story. Think about the facts it gives you. You may want to write down the facts.
- Think about what you already know. Make a guess by putting together what you know and what you've read.

Challenge Yourself

Try this special challenge. Read each story. Answer the question. Then write one more inference you can make.

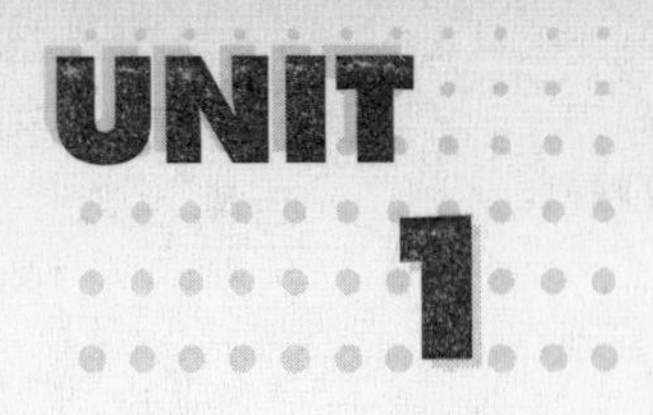

1. In 1755 France had troops in Ohio. England sent troops to fight the French. The English army could not march through the thick forests. Day after day they cut down trees to make a road. They made much noise. Their red uniforms made them easy to see. The French soon found the English troops. The French troops attacked. More than half of the English troops were killed.

2. The Blues moved the ball down the field. One player kicked it to another. The Reds could not take the ball away. The Blues got closer to the net. The Red's goalie caught one of the balls that was kicked into the net. But she did not catch the next one. The Blues scored still another point.

3. The whooping crane is one of two kinds of cranes that live in North America. It is a large bird with a long neck and long legs. Long ago these cranes lived on the grasslands. Then people moved to these places. The people took the land where these cranes had made homes. The cranes began to disappear. At one point there were just 21 cranes left. Then people started to help these cranes. They gave them space to build nests. They helped keep the cranes safe.

4. The Smithsonian is a big museum. The bones of animals that lived long ago are kept there. You can also see clothes, tools, and cars that people have used in the past. The first United States rocket is there, too.

______ **1.** Which of these sentences is probably true?

A. The English attacked the French.
B. The French helped the English build a road.
C. The French won the battle.

______ **2.** Which of these sentences is probably true?

A. The Blues were beating the Reds.
B. The Reds needed more players.
C. The Blues were sore losers.

______ **3.** Which of these sentences is probably true?

A. People found that the cranes needed help.
B. People used whooping cranes for food.
C. No whooping cranes are left today.

______ **4.** Which of these sentences is probably true?

A. The Smithsonian sells cars.
B. You can learn about the past at the Smithsonian.
C. The Smithsonian has live animals.

UNIT 2

1. Long ago a man named Zenger owned a small newspaper. It was called the *New York Weekly Journal*. Zenger wrote a story about the English governor. The governor was mad. He said Zenger did not write the truth about him. The governor took Zenger to court and charged him with lying. The court said Zenger was not guilty.

2. Yeast is a tiny plant. It is mixed with sugar, flour, and warm water to make bread dough. When the dough is put in a warm place, the yeast makes it rise. It gets larger as it rises. After the dough rises, you must punch it down. Then you form it into a loaf and put it into the oven. The dough rises again when you bake it.

3. Much money must be spent to keep roads safe. In the winter snow and ice must be plowed away. In the summer the cracks and holes made in the roads during the winter must be fixed. Tax money is used to take care of some roads. But tax dollars are not used to fix toll roads. Money for toll roads comes from each car or truck that uses the road.

4. You don't need a friend when you play catch with a boomerang. A boomerang can come back to you when you throw it. A boomerang is a flat piece of wood. It looks like a wide vee. The arms are shaped like two jet wings. When you throw it, air pushes up and over the arms. This keeps it in the air. If you throw it the right way, you can make it travel about half a block before it returns.

______ **1.** Which of these sentences is probably true?

A. The court believed Zenger's story was true.
B. The governor was fired by the king.
C. The governor sold Zenger's printing press.

______ **2.** Which of these sentences is probably true?

A. Yeast makes bread dough hard.
B. Heat and yeast make bread dough rise.
C. Brown bread does not have yeast.

______ **3.** Which of these sentences is probably true?

A. Most highways get money from tolls.
B. Weather can hurt roads.
C. Only trucks pay to use a toll road.

______ **4.** Which of these sentences is probably true?

A. Boomerangs are mostly used as toys.
B. Boomerangs can carry messages.
C. Boomerangs need to be carried by two people.

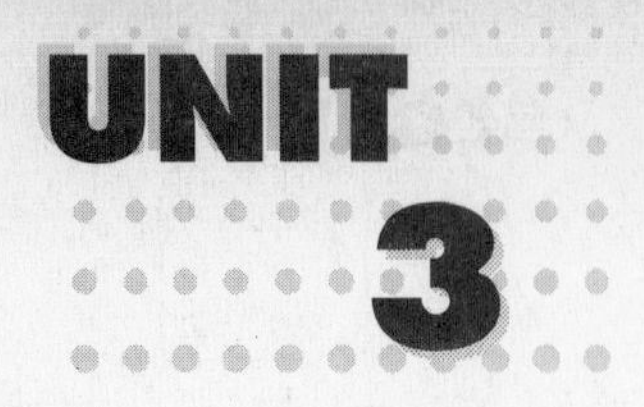

1. One orange is left in the bowl. You touch and smell it. The orange feels soft and mushy. It has a sharp smell. Part of the skin is broken. There is something white and powdery on the skin. You decide not to eat the orange.

---

2. The Brooklyn Bridge links Brooklyn and Manhattan in New York. It is very long. The bridge hangs from long steel cables that are 16 inches thick. Two huge towers hold up the cables. The bridge has six lanes for cars and trucks.

---

3. American settlers had a hard time moving west. They had to travel over mountains and through thick forests. For years they followed small trails made by Native Americans. In 1811 the government made one of the trails into a road. People could then go all the way from Maryland to Illinois. You can still travel from Washington, D.C., to St. Louis, Missouri, on this road.

---

4. Terns are sea birds that are like gulls. A tern is about 15 inches long. It is a strong flier. One kind of tern flies from the North Pole to the South Pole and back each year. Terns eat fish. They build nests near coasts.

______ **1.** Which of these sentences is probably true?

A. Eating the orange may make you sick.
B. The orange is not ripe yet.
C. The orange should be used for juice.

______ **2.** Which of these statements is probably true?

A. The bridge can hold many cars and trucks.
B. The Brooklyn Bridge is the world's largest bridge.
C. The bridge is never used by people.

______ **3.** Which of these sentences is probably true?

A. Some roads were once small trails.
B. Roads are hard to build.
C. Native Americans helped build the road.

______ **4.** Which of these sentences is probably true?

A. Terns live near the middle of the earth.
B. Terns can fly long distances.
C. Terns lay three eggs each year.

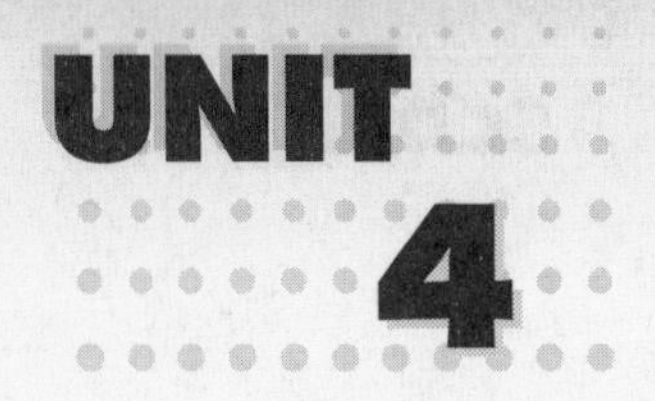

1. “Leave the hall light on, please,” Luis called. “And please don’t close the door.” Luis’s mom and dad had gone out. Tía Rosa was putting Luis to bed.

2. The Constitution has all the laws of the United States. It tells what people can and cannot do. It tells what states can and cannot do. The Constitution also tells about the duties of the president. It tells how people can pass new laws. It tells whose job it is to see that the laws are followed.

3. A lake is a body of water. Lakes are surrounded on all sides by land. A gulf is a body of water that is not surrounded by land on all sides. A gulf opens into an ocean. Because of this a gulf is much like an ocean. Gulfs can be deep. Ocean fish live in gulfs. So do ocean shellfish. Two big gulfs touch North America.

4. A long time ago, people in America had a king. The king lived in England. He told people in America how to live and work. They didn’t like the king. He made them pay a tax for a war they did not fight. The Americans did not want to pay the tax.

______ **1.** Which of these sentences is probably true?

A. Luis is afraid of the dark.
B. Luis's mom and dad will be back in a week.
C. It is time for Luis to eat.

______ **2.** Which of these sentences is probably true?

A. The Constitution affects people in the United States.
B. The President writes the Constitution.
C. The Constitution cannot be changed.

______ **3.** Which of these sentences is probably true?

A. Ocean plants can live in a gulf.
B. Gulfs are sometimes lakes.
C. Fishing isn't safe in a gulf.

______ **4.** Which of these sentences is probably true?

A. Americans gladly helped the English king.
B. Americans thought that the tax was unfair.
C. Americans still have a king.

UNIT 5

1. Holland is a country that is next to the sea. Dikes, or walls, are built around the towns in Holland. The walls keep the sea from flooding the towns. One day a boy saw a small hole in the dike near his town. Sea water was running out of the hole. And the hole was getting bigger. He put his finger in the hole and called for help. He waited a long time. Finally some people came to help. At last the boy could go home. He knew that the town was safe.

2. Shree walked to the ticket counter. She waited in line. Five other people were buying tickets. She heard people asking for seats. Some talked about left field. Others said, "One near first base." One person said, "Behind home plate."

3. Train tracks have signals to keep the trains from hitting each other. The train track is divided into blocks. Electricity flows through each block of track. When a train moves along the track, it runs over a switch. The switch turns on a red light. A train coming from another direction sees the red light. It stops so the two trains will not crash into each other.

4. The sun was warm. There was not a cloud in the sky. The lilacs smelled sweet. Chris and his friend started to play catch. They were very happy. Spring was finally here. They played catch all afternoon. Then Chris thought, "Oh, no! I had a trumpet lesson today."

SCORE

______ **1.** Which of these sentences is probably true?

A. The people fixed the hole.
B. The boy fixed the hole by himself.
C. The people thought the boy was silly.

______ **2.** Which of these sentences is probably true?

A. Shree was going on a train trip.
B. Shree was buying a ticket to the baseball game.
C. Shree was in line at the movie theater.

______ **3.** Which of these sentences is probably true?

A. Trains obey the signals.
B. Red lights always mean "go".
C. Trains always go the same way.

______ **4.** Which of these sentences is probably true?

A. Chris ran to school after playing catch.
B. Chris liked winter better than spring.
C. Chris missed his trumpet lesson.

1. Kim gets up and goes out for the paper every morning. Then she eats breakfast and reads the comics with her mom. One day the paper stopped coming. It did not come for a week. Kim and her mom wondered what was wrong. Then Kim's mom found an envelope that was addressed to the paper. She had forgotten to mail it.

---

2. A drug is something that causes a change in the body. Medicines are drugs that can help parts of the body work better. Medicines can make people feel better when they are sick. But some kinds of drugs can hurt the body. Some drugs make the heart work too fast or too slow. Some drugs make people act in ways that are not safe. Certain drugs can cause death.

---

3. Bill got on his bike. He rode down the street past homes and trees. Then he reached the park. There he put on his shin pads and his cleats. He began kicking the round ball back and forth between his feet.

---

4. In 1895 a man named Marconi sent the first radio code signal through the air. This early radio was called a "wireless." That meant it sent sound over a space without using wires. The first radios were put on ships. They helped save people who were lost at sea. It was the "wireless" that saved some people on the sinking *Titanic*.

______ **1.** Which of these sentences is probably true?

A. Kim's mom had not paid the bill for the paper.
B. A new person was delivering the paper.
C. Kim's mom had paid for the paper.

______ **2.** Which of these sentences is probably true?

A. People should never use medicines.
B. Medicines should be used with care.
C. All medicines make people sick.

______ **3.** Which of these sentences is probably true?

A. Bill went to play soccer.
B. Bill went to his job after school.
C. Bill was on an errand for his grandmother.

______ **4.** Which of these sentences is probably true?

A. Radio was first used to help ships in trouble.
B. Marconi gave speeches on his radio.
C. The first radio station was set up in Chicago.

UNIT 7

1. Juan worked after school at a small shop. He made deliveries for the owner. One day the owner told Juan to make a delivery. Juan looked at the box. It had his address on it. Juan asked, "Is this right?" The owner told Juan to take the box to that address. When Juan got to the address, all his friends were there. They sang "Happy Birthday" to Juan.

---

2. Cars use gasoline for fuel. When the fuel burns, a harmful gas goes into the air. The gas is carbon dioxide. A car gives off other harmful gases, too. These gases make the air all over the earth dirty. In some places it is not safe for some people to breathe. Dirty air hurts their lungs. It can cause heart problems.

---

3. Jim Thorpe was a star athlete. Playing sports was easy for him. He played baseball and football. He also won medals for running track at the Olympic games.

---

4. Bill and his dad got into the car. They were going to the store. They backed out of the driveway. Both of them heard a noise in the back of the car. As they drove, the noise got louder. The car bumped up and down. They pulled over and stopped the car. When they stepped out of the car, they noticed that it sagged to one side.

______ **1.** Which of these sentences is probably true?

A. The owner wanted to celebrate Juan's birthday.
B. Juan didn't get along well with the owner.
C. Juan got the job through a class at school.

______ **2.** Which of these sentences is probably true?

A. Cars can make the air dirty.
B. Dirty air is good for your lungs.
C. Cars help clean the air.

______ **3.** Which of these sentences is probably true?

A. Track is harder than baseball.
B. Baseball was Thorpe's best sport.
C. Thorpe could play more than one sport.

______ **4.** Which of these sentences is probably true?

A. Bill and his dad rode on a motorcycle.
B. The car was wet.
C. The car had a flat tire.

UNIT 8

1. Brown Bear was a Delaware Indian. He learned to hunt from his father. Brown Bear and his father hunted for food. His mother and sister followed them. They were gone for many days. After the hunt the family fixed the meat of the animals they killed. They made clothes and tents from the skins of the animals. They made tools from the bones and other parts.

2. Have you heard traffic news today? It may have come from a person in a helicopter high above the city. A helicopter has blades on the top of it. It does not have wings. The blades spin fast. Then air rushes up and over the blades. The moving air pushes the helicopter straight up. When it's time to land, the helicopter can come straight down.

3. Look around. Do you see something made of bricks? People have built things with bricks for thousands of years. Old bricks have been found all over the world. Most bricks are made of clay. The clay is mixed with water to make a stiff mud. Then the bricks are shaped and baked. Today bricks are used to build houses. In the past, bricks were also used to make streets.

4. Colin's dog goes everywhere with Colin. The dog takes Colin where he wants to go. Colin holds onto the dog's leash, and the dog leads him. When the dog stops, Colin stops. When the dog goes forward, Colin goes, too.

______ **1.** Which of these sentences is probably true?

A. The Delaware lived only on fish.
B. Brown Bear taught himself to hunt.
C. A Delaware Indian family worked together.

______ **2.** Which of these sentences is probably true?

A. Helicopters don't fly very well.
B. Few people ever ride in helicopters.
C. Helicopters can land and take off in small spaces.

______ **3.** Which of these sentences is probably true?

A. People do not use bricks anymore.
B. Early Americans built many things with bricks they made.
C. Bricks were first used on streets.

______ **4.** Which of these sentences is probably true?

A. Colin's dog is not very smart.
B. Colin needs to be in a wheelchair.
C. Colin's dog is a guide dog.

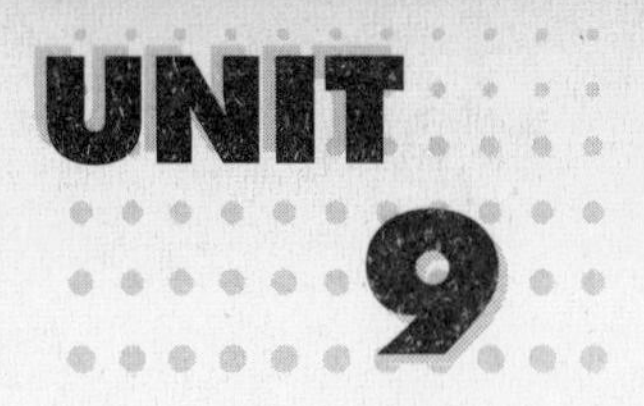

1. May was on the road. She saw a plane over her car. It was a warm day, and the windows were rolled down. May heard the plane's engine go off and then on. This happened many times. The plane turned and came in low over the road. The plane turned again. May pulled off the road.

---

2. When a ship goes from New York City to Cape Town, South Africa, it must cross the line that divides the earth. This line is called the equator. It divides north and south. When the ship crosses this line, people on the ship have a party. Everyone who is crossing this line for the first time must do tricks. When they all have had a turn, the party ends.

---

3. The Tennessee River runs through high hills. For years the river flooded. Water ran over the banks of the river. The water ruined fields and houses. People built a high dam. Water collected behind the dam. This made a lake. When it rained, the floodwater went into the lake.

---

4. After World War II, Berlin was divided into two parts. The parts were East and West Berlin. Even though Berlin was split this way, people could move from one part to the other. For many years people left East Berlin to live in West Berlin. The government in East Berlin did not want people to leave. They built a wall between the two parts.

______ **1.** Which of these sentences is probably true?

A. May was waiting for her mother.
B. The plane had problems and needed to land.
C. The pilot was counting the cars on the road.

______ **2.** Which of these sentences is probably true?

A. The equator is a row of cans in the ocean.
B. A ship cannot go from New York to Cape Town.
C. The equator is an important line.

______ **3.** Which of these sentences is probably true?

A. The Tennessee River dried up.
B. Dams help stop flooding.
C. River water is not safe to drink.

______ **4.** Which of these sentences is probably true?

A. The wall kept people from leaving East Berlin.
B. People usually went to West Berlin for vacation.
C. Berlin wasn't divided into parts.

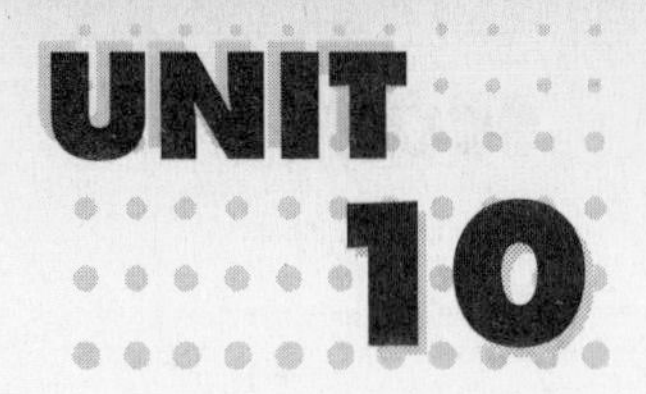

1. All birds do not have the same kind of beaks. Some birds have short, strong beaks. These birds eat seeds. They can crack open the seeds and eat them. Some birds eat insects. These birds must have beaks that help them get to insects in the ground and inside tree trunks.

2. Thousands of people lived in New Orleans in 1830. All around the town were swamps. Mosquitoes lived in the swamps. People began to get sick and die. They died from a disease called yellow fever. More and more people died. It took a long time for doctors to learn that the mosquitoes gave people yellow fever.

3. Jazz is a kind of music. People first played jazz in America. When people play jazz, they make up the songs as they play. This makes jazz seem new all the time.

4. First you need to make the ground ready. Break up the big pieces of dirt with a hoe. Use a shovel to take out all the rocks. Make sure there are no weeds or grass in the dirt. Then make straight lines in the dirt. Poke little holes in the lines. Keep the holes about one inch apart. Next put seeds in the holes.

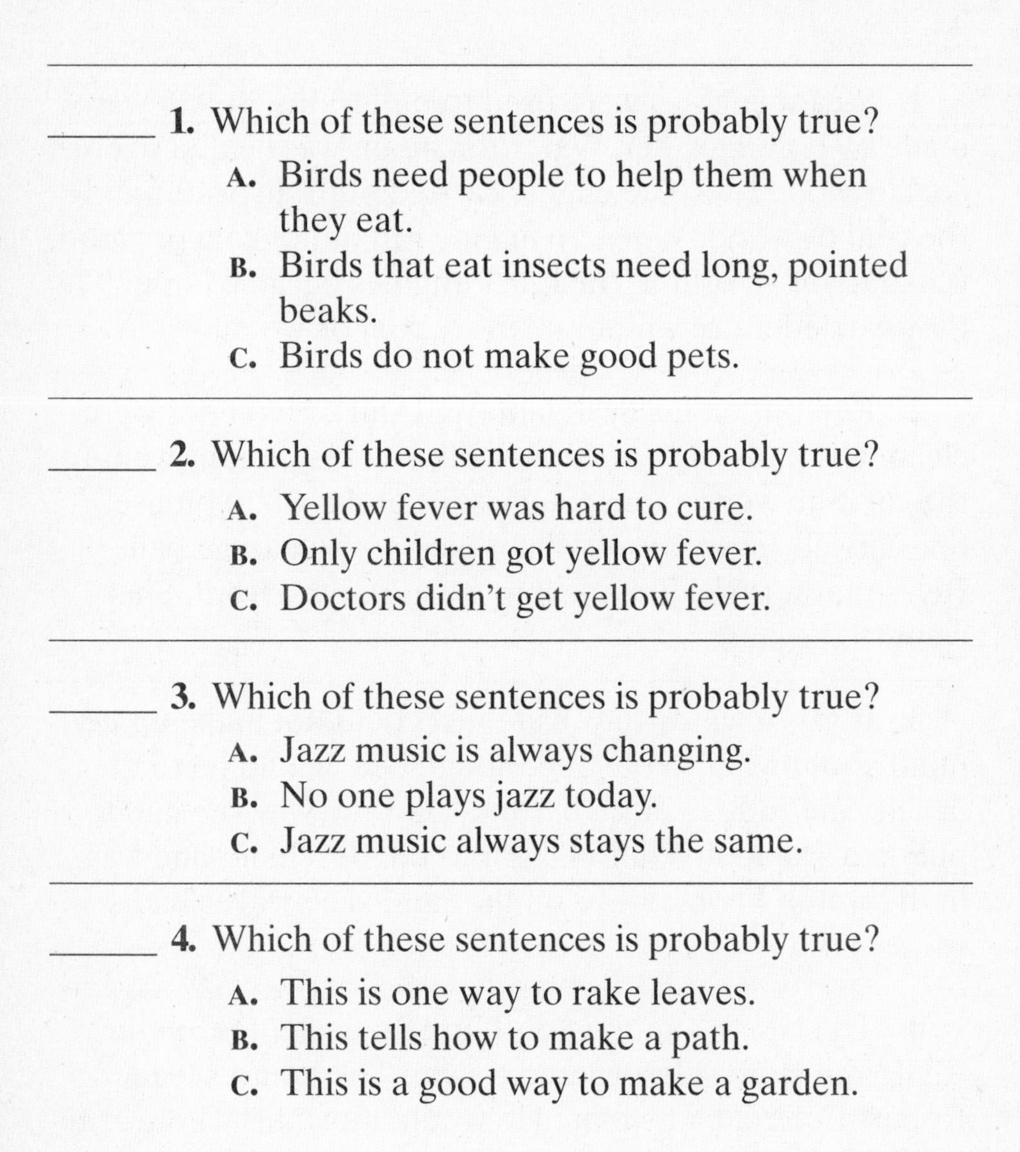

_____ **1.** Which of these sentences is probably true?

A. Birds need people to help them when they eat.

B. Birds that eat insects need long, pointed beaks.

C. Birds do not make good pets.

_____ **2.** Which of these sentences is probably true?

A. Yellow fever was hard to cure.

B. Only children got yellow fever.

C. Doctors didn't get yellow fever.

_____ **3.** Which of these sentences is probably true?

A. Jazz music is always changing.

B. No one plays jazz today.

C. Jazz music always stays the same.

_____ **4.** Which of these sentences is probably true?

A. This is one way to rake leaves.

B. This tells how to make a path.

C. This is a good way to make a garden.

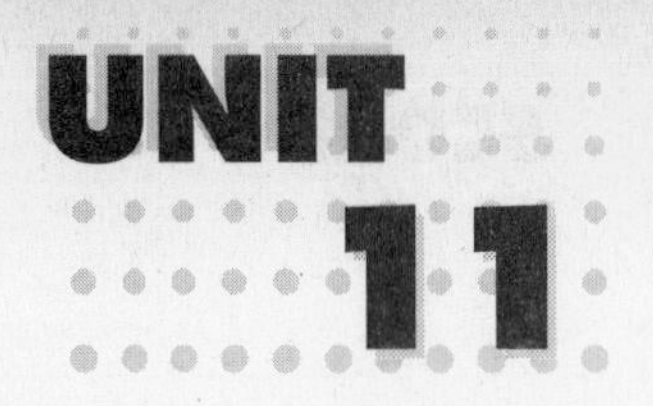

1. Steam engines were used to pull trains. Steam was made by boiling water. Water for steam was heated over a coal or wood fire. The engine carried both the water and the coal or wood. When an engine ran out of coal or wood, it had to move off the track. As engines became larger, they carried more water and more coal or wood.

2. Ben put on his best pants and shirt. His shoes were clean. His nails were scrubbed. He and his mother went to the car. She wore a long, black skirt and a white blouse. She carried some music. When they got to a large hall, Ben's mother told him to sit in a chair at the front. She went to the stage.

3. It was a windy day. Kate just could not make up her mind about what to do. She thought she would go to the beach. She rode over on her bike. On the way she had to put on a sweater. When she got to the beach, no one was in the water. People were on the sand. The waves had white tops.

4. The North and the South fought each other in the Civil War. Both sides wanted to win. The South's leader, Robert E. Lee, had a plan. He would move his whole army north. As Lee's army moved, the army from the North followed it. Both armies fought in a small town called Gettysburg. After three days Lee's army could not fight anymore.

SCORE

______ **1.** Which of these sentences is probably true?

A. Bigger engines needed more fuel.
B. Steam engines are still used today.
C. Steam engines were also used in cars.

______ **2.** Which of these sentences is probably true?

A. Ben's mother will play music in a show.
B. Ben didn't like music.
C. Ben's mom always took him on rides with her.

______ **3.** Which of these sentences is probably true?

A. Kate went to the beach in a car.
B. The wind made it too cold to swim.
C. No one was on the beach.

______ **4.** Which of these sentences is probably true?

A. Lee's army won the fight.
B. The army from the North ran away.
C. Lee's army lost the fight.

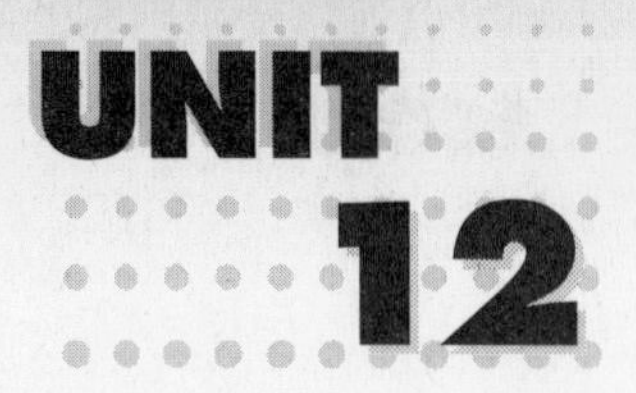

1. Both John Adams and Thomas Jefferson were presidents. When they were young, they were not friends. Adams thought people should live in cities. He thought they should make things for other people. Jefferson thought people should be farmers. As both men grew older, they began to agree on things. They became good friends. Both men died the same year on the Fourth of July.

2. In the past, people used gas lamps to light their homes. Gas for the lights came into a house through a pipe. People cooked food on stoves that burned wood or coal. Then Robert Bunsen made a gas burner. His burner was put on a stove. People hooked up the new stove to their gas pipes.

3. The *Titanic* was a large passenger ship. People said it was built so well that it could not sink. They said nothing could hurt it. During its first trip, it hit an iceberg. The ice cut a hole in the side of the ship. The ship filled with water and sank.

4. It was Jill's turn to bring snacks to school. This time she planned to bring a special snack. She made a cupcake for everyone. She put a little candy on each cake. She also put a tiny candle on each cake. She hoped the class would sing after the teacher lit the candles.

______ **1.** Which of these sentences is probably true?

A. Jefferson did not want to live in the city.
B. Both men thought people should be farmers.
C. Adams never liked Jefferson.

______ **2.** Which of these sentences is probably true?

A. Bunsen found another use for gas.
B. Bunsen discovered gas.
C. Wood or coal costs less than gas.

______ **3.** Which of these sentences is probably true?

A. The ship was the largest ever built.
B. People were surprised when the ship sank.
C. The ship was the fastest ever built.

______ **4.** Which of these sentences is probably true?

A. It was Jill's birthday.
B. The teacher told her to bring cake.
C. Jill was tired of school food.

UNIT 13

1. Faith Ringgold is an artist. She cuts shapes out of cloth. Then she sews them together to make quilts. The pieces of cloth in her quilts have many patterns. She often paints pictures on pieces of the cloth. She tells stories about her life on her quilts. *Tar Beach* is the name of one of her quilts. It tells a story about a place where she spent time when she was a child.

---

2. How does sand end up on a beach? Grains of sand were once part of large rocks. Very slowly ice and heat made the rocks break down into small pieces. Wind and water carried the pieces away from the rocks. The force of the wind and water wore the pieces into the smooth, tiny grains you see on beaches.

---

3. Dad slowed down. The truck ahead was going much slower than the rest of the cars. Dad could not pass it. The truck was going down the middle of the road. A bucket of yellow paint hung off the back of the truck. A brush dipped in and out. The brush left paint on the road.

---

4. There used to be wild camels in West Texas. The Army brought the camels from Africa. The camels could travel long distances without water. So the Army used them to carry big loads. But the camels were hard to manage. They spit at the drivers and bit them. Many camels ran away and were never found.

______ **1.** Which of these sentences is probably true?

A. *Tar Beach* tells a story about Ringgold's dog.
B. Stories are not only found in books.
C. A quilt is made of paper.

______ **2.** Which of these sentences is probably true?

A. It takes a long time to make sand.
B. Sand is always hot.
C. Water and wind cannot move sand.

______ **3.** Which of these sentences is probably true?

A. The truck was slowing down traffic.
B. The truck was trimming trees.
C. Dad raced around the truck.

______ **4.** Which of these sentences is probably true?

A. The camels could carry only small loads.
B. The Army still uses camels in West Texas.
C. The camels that ran away became wild.

UNIT 14

1. Ann saw two little heads looking out of the attic window. “Oh, no!” she said. “Not again.” The heads each had a pointed nose and long whiskers. Each one looked as if it were wearing a black mask. Tiny claws scratched at the glass. Then Ann saw a big raccoon jump from a tree onto the roof.

---

2. A 17-year locust has a long life. It spends 17 years underground as a worm, or nymph. For many years it eats, sleeps, and grows. When it is time, the nymph comes up out of the ground and sheds its brown shell. When its shell is gone, the locust can spread its new wings. But it only lives a few weeks as an adult. During that time it lays eggs in the twigs of trees and shrubs. The eggs hatch, and the small nymphs drop from the twigs and go into the ground.

---

3. The street was closed to cars. Hundreds of people were standing on both sides of the street. Some of them had brought chairs to sit on. Children were running back and forth. They wanted to see what was coming. Some people waved flags. Then the band began to play. Everyone hoped to see someone they knew march by.

---

4. The long, gray wall in town looked bad. The town asked the school to help. Children from grades one and two picked up trash at the wall. Those in grades three and four planted a garden there. The artists in grades five and six painted pictures on the wall. The pictures told a story about the town's past.

______ **1.** Which of these sentences is probably true?

A. Raccoons have babies called lambs.
B. Ann can't keep raccoons out of the attic.
C. Kittens chase raccoons.

______ **2.** Which of these sentences is probably true?

A. A locust changes while it is in the ground.
B. Locusts live only underground.
C. A locust can fly when it is a nymph.

______ **3.** Which of these sentences is probably true?

A. Everyone stood in the middle of the street.
B. People were waiting for a parade.
C. The children all stayed in one place.

______ **4.** Which of these sentences is probably true?

A. The children worked together to make the wall pretty.
B. No one wanted to help the children.
C. The pictures on the wall did not tell a story.

UNIT 15

1. Oil is a resource. So are coal and gas. They are fuels. We burn these fuels to make heat and power. We use gas and oil to run our cars. All three of these resources come from the earth. They were formed long before people lived on the earth.

---

2. In the 1800s a man from France wanted people all over the world to know that America stood for freedom. He asked an artist friend to help him. First the artist drew a picture of a woman wearing a long robe. He showed the woman holding a torch and wearing a crown. The statue was finished in 1885. Now it stands on Liberty Island. It has greeted many people who have come to America.

---

3. Even though she didn't speak, I knew Mom was mad. Her face was red. Her hands were on her hips. She was standing in the door, tapping her foot. I was late again. I tried to run up to my room fast.

---

4. The two children lay on their backs in the grass. They were looking up at the sky. "I see a whale. See him spout!" said one. "That doesn't look like a whale," said the other. "It looks like an elephant." Neither could agree on the shapes they saw.

______ **1.** Which of these sentences is probably true?

A. No one uses resources.
B. Oil, gas, and coal are not resources.
C. Oil, coal, and gas help people to meet needs.

______ **2.** Which of these sentences is probably true?

A. The man's statue was never finished.
B. The statue is The Statue of Liberty.
C. The statue stands for all artists.

______ **3.** Which of these sentences is probably true?

A. Mom was pleased with me.
B. People can say things without using words.
C. Mom shouted, and I knew she was mad.

______ **4.** Which of these sentences is probably true?

A. The children were watching cartoons outside.
B. An elephant was riding a whale.
C. The children were seeing shapes in the clouds.

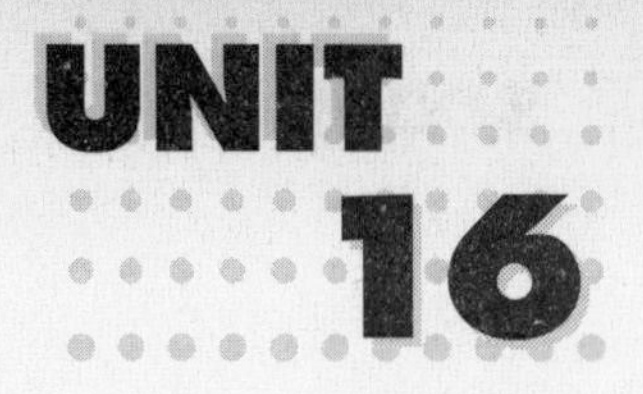

1. How is the air heated in a hot-air balloon? Pilots use a gas flame to heat the air. If a pilot wants to go up, he or she shoots the flame up into the balloon. This makes the air hot. The pilot must cool the air to go down. Once the balloon is up, the wind guides the balloon. If there is no wind, the balloon stays in one place.

---

2. Some insects have built-in ways to hide from their enemies. One insect looks just like a stick. Its body is long, thin, and brown. Its legs are very thin. When birds see it, they think it is a twig. So they don't eat it. Another insect looks like a leaf. It is green and flat, and it hangs on a plant. Birds think it is part of the plant.

---

3. We put all the books away in boxes. The teacher took our little bits of crayon and threw them away. She put our big ones in a box. Some children took the pictures off the walls. I washed the chalkboard. The janitor came in to lock the windows. The teacher put her plants in a box to take home.

---

4. Some words sound just alike. Sometimes this can cause trouble. Suppose someone asks you to pick up rocks with a crane. What should you do? Do you use a bird with a long neck? Or do you use a machine? How will you know which crane to use?

______ **1.** Which of these sentences is probably true?

A. Hot air makes the balloon rise.
B. Balloons get you places fast.
C. Hot-air balloons fly with wings.

______ **2.** Which of these sentences is probably true?

A. Birds are not very smart.
B. Some insects are shaped like parts of plants.
C. Insects love to play tricks.

______ **3.** Which of these sentences is probably true?

A. It is the first day of school.
B. It is the last day of school.
C. There has been a fire at school.

______ **4.** Which of these sentences is probably true?

A. Words can sound alike but have different meanings.
B. *Crane* and *crane* do not sound the same.
C. All words have the same meaning.

1. Long ago, life was hard for the settlers who lived on the prairie. Often they lived far away from other people. So there wasn't much help if there was trouble. They had to make homes out of dirt because there weren't many trees. And there were always wild animals that roamed the prairie. The settlers had to raise all their own food. But sometimes it didn't rain for months, and all their crops died.

2. Jack looked up. He saw the same thing he had seen each day this week. The geese were flying south. He heard them honking as they went. "Too bad," he thought. "It will soon be cold and snowy. I'll have to play inside."

3. Maria did not look up when the teacher spoke. She did not hear what she was supposed to do with the paper. She walked to the teacher's desk to ask. She watched the teacher's lips as he spoke. When the teacher turned his head and spoke, Maria did not hear what he said.

4. There are several ways to help a forest that is quickly losing its trees. One way is to plant young trees, or seedlings. These trees replace those that die or are cut down. And they grow quickly. Sometimes people fly over a forest and drop seeds. New trees will sprout from these seeds.

______ **1.** Which of these sentences is probably true?

- **A.** The settlers were brave people.
- **B.** The prairie was always wet and muddy.
- **C.** The settlers shopped for food in the East.

______ **2.** Which of these sentences is probably true?

- **A.** The geese spoke with Jack about the weather.
- **B.** Flying geese can mean a change of season.
- **C.** Jack works in a birdhouse.

______ **3.** Which of these sentences is probably true?

- **A.** Maria needs to be a better listener.
- **B.** Maria cannot see the paper.
- **C.** Maria reads lips to understand people.

______ **4.** Which of these sentences is probably true?

- **A.** It is important to keep forests from dying.
- **B.** Trees never die in a forest.
- **C.** People don't really care about forests.

UNIT 18

1. Kate counted out five pairs of socks. She put one extra pair in the pile. She found the T-shirt she liked to sleep in. She chose some shorts and shirts. "Don't forget your teddy bear," her dad called.

2. Your skin is made of a thick layer of tiny, living parts called cells. Your skin helps keep you alive. It holds in the moisture that your body must have. Sometimes skin from one part of the body can be put onto another part. This is called a skin graft. Skin grafts can help someone who has had a bad burn.

3. A cave is a hole under the ground. Most caves are formed in rock called limestone. Caves are made by water. Water eats away part of the rock. Over many years a small hole or crack in a rock becomes very big. Then it becomes a home for bears or bats. And it becomes a place people want to explore.

4. Could you buy a candy bar today with a seashell? No. But long ago, people used seashells as money. In Africa, you could buy a goat for one hundred seashells. You can still find these shells on the beach. They are about the size of a bean. But don't try to buy a candy bar with them. They're not worth a penny.

______ **1.** Which of these sentences is probably true?

A. Kate wants to see how many socks she has.
B. Kate doesn't like nightgowns.
C. Kate is getting ready for a trip.

______ **2.** Which of these sentences is probably true?

A. Skin grafts don't work.
B. Skin grows on only one part of the body.
C. A skin graft can save a person's life.

______ **3.** Which of these sentences is probably true?

A. Water collects in limestone cracks.
B. Animals stay away from caves.
C. Caves are open to the sun.

______ **4.** Which of these sentences is probably true?

A. Long ago it was good to have many seashells.
B. Today people shop with seashells.
C. Wood is made from seashells.

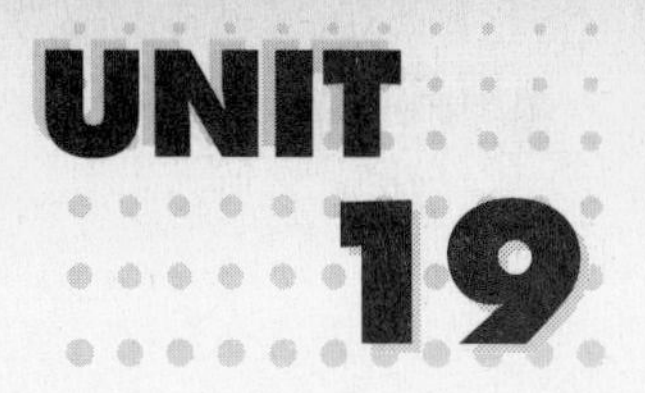

1. The Incas lived long ago in South America. They were the first people to grow white potatoes. They used them to make bread. People from Spain came to the Incas' home. When these people left, they took the white potatoes home with them to Europe. They became the main food for many people there. When the English came to North America, they brought the potatoes back across the sea.

2. Don and his dad walked into the bank. "Where does a bank get money?" Don asked. "The bank gets money from people like us," Dad said. "We put money into a savings account. Then the bank uses that money to cash checks or make loans to people. The bank's money comes from all the money that people put into bank accounts."

3. Long ago, people made furniture, clothes, and tools at home. Each family worked together to make a certain thing. If you wanted to buy a table, you went to a family who made tables. Back then it took a long time to make things. Now tables, dresses, and other things are made quickly in factories. Then they are shipped to a store. You don't have to wait for what you want. You can just go in and buy it.

4. A large truck pulled up into the driveway. Four men got out of the truck. They pushed up the back door and rolled a large, black object off the truck. It had a set of white keys on one end. Two men pushed it, and two men pulled it. When it was in the house, they screwed on three legs. Four men lifted it so that it was right-side up. One man sat down to play a song.

______ **1.** Which of these sentences is probably true?

A. Potatoes can grow well in different places.
B. The Spanish grew the first white potatoes.
C. White potatoes taste like sweet potatoes.

______ **2.** Which of these sentences is probably true?

A. The bank uses your money for many things.
B. Banks print the money they lend.
C. The government takes the bank's money.

______ **3.** Which of these sentences is probably true?

A. Things are made faster at home than in a factory.
B. People come to your home to make things.
C. Today most things are not made at home.

______ **4.** Which of these sentences is probably true?

A. Playing the piano is easy for everyone.
B. No one wants to move a piano.
C. It takes at least four people to move a piano.

UNIT 20

1. Eskimo sculpture is beautiful. People come from all around to buy it. They like the simple animal shapes that the Eskimos carve out of soapstone or animal bones. Eskimos carve the shapes of the animals that live around them.

2. The spring was very wet. A pond formed in the field. Children playing in the field saw a duck swimming in the pond. Soon it warmed up, and the pond dried up. The duck came back to the pond with some baby ducks. But there was no water. The children brought out a plastic swimming pool. They filled the pool with water. The mother duck jumped in, but the babies could not.

3. Frank rode his horse as fast as he could. He swung his lasso above his head. The cows were running all around him. It was very dusty. Frank's dad was standing at the fence. The gate to the corral was open.

4. There are two kinds of rocket fuel. The oldest kind is solid. It was first made long ago by people in China. They placed it in a tube in a rocket. Then they lit it. The fuel exploded. And the rocket went up into the air. The newer fuel is a liquid. It is used more often than the solid fuel. But it works the same way. It is put in a box at the bottom of the rocket. It explodes, and the rocket goes into the air.

______ **1.** Which of these sentences is probably true?

A. The Eskimos make art from nature.
B. You can wash with soapstone.
C. Eskimos are not good artists.

______ **2.** Which of these sentences is probably true?

A. The babies couldn't jump over the side of the pool.
B. The mother duck didn't want the babies to swim.
C. Many people don't like ducks.

______ **3.** Which of these sentences is probably true?

A. Frank was herding the cows to the corral.
B. The cows needed some exercise.
C. Frank was the winner in a horse race.

______ **4.** Which of these sentences is probably true?

A. Rocket fuel has been used for a long time.
B. A rocket costs much money to build.
C. Rockets fly around the earth.

UNIT 21

1. Every country makes money for people to use. People use coins that are made from metals. Coins might be silver or copper. Gold is too soft for a coin. People use paper money. Paper money might have pictures of kings, queens, or buildings on it. A check is a kind of money, too. A check means you have money in a bank to pay for what you buy.

2. Beth wanted to find out where her aunt lived. She looked at a map. She found the name of the town. Then she saw a star by the town. Her teacher told her that a star meant the town was the capital of the state. Beth looked at other states on the map. Each state had one town that was marked by a star.

3. Sea turtles come out of the water to lay their eggs. The female turtle comes up on the beach when it is dark and no one is there. She digs a hole in the sand. She lays the eggs in the hole and covers them with sand. Then she goes back into the water. The baby turtles hatch in a few weeks. They hurry to get into the water.

4. Mom mixed the sugar and the butter. She added flour and nuts. She was making my favorite cookies. She shaped them into balls. She made each one flat with a fork. Then she put them into the oven. Just then the telephone rang. It was her sister. They talked and talked. I began to smell something bad. I heard Mom yell, "Oh, no!"

______ **1.** Which of these sentences is probably true?

A. Money looks different in different countries.
B. Silver coins are the only kind of money.
C. A check is not as good as money.

______ **2.** Which of these sentences is probably true?

A. Each state has two capitals.
B. Each state has one capital.
C. Some states don't have capitals.

______ **3.** Which of these sentences is probably true?

A. The mother sea turtle never sees her babies.
B. Mother sea turtles live on land.
C. Sea turtles stay to watch the eggs hatch.

______ **4.** Which of these sentences is probably true?

A. Mom's sister said something silly.
B. The cookies were burning in the oven.
C. The cookies fell out of the oven.

UNIT 22

1. Bud and his dad took turns mowing the grass. They tried to cut it once each week. They used a mower with a sharp blade. After many weeks the grass began to look uneven after it was mowed. It was high in some places and low in other places. Bud looked at the blade. It was dull and needed to be sharpened.

---

2. A dirt road changes over time. When it rains, water washes away some of the dirt. The road becomes very wet and muddy. Cars get stuck in the mud. They make big holes as they try to get out. When the road dries, it has big holes in it. When the weather is hot and dry, the dirt on the road cracks. Some of it blows away.

---

3. Sam built a fence in his yard. He dug eight deep holes. He put a post in each hole. The posts would hold up the boards for the fence. Sam laid a board across the top of the posts. He used a special tool to see if the posts were all the same height. The tool was called a level. Sam did not start putting on the boards until the level showed that each post was the same height. He wanted the fence to look just right.

---

4. In the fall the leaves fall off the trees onto the roof. Often they get stuck in the gutters. A gutter on a house catches rain as it runs off the roof. The gutter takes the rain away from the house. The rain runs down a pipe to the ground. If a gutter is filled with leaves, rain does not run away from the house. The gutters fill up, and the water spills over.

______ **1.** Which of these sentences is probably true?

A. Bud watched his dad cut the grass all year.
B. Water made the blade get rusty.
C. A sharp blade on a mower cuts grass evenly.

______ **2.** Which of these sentences is probably true?

A. Weather can change a dirt road.
B. Water helps a dirt road stay smooth.
C. Muddy roads are fun to drive on.

______ **3.** Which of these sentences is probably true?

A. A fence should always be painted.
B. A level helps you see if things are even.
C. It is easy to make a fence.

______ **4.** Which of these sentences is probably true?

A. Gutters hold water for plants.
B. Things on a roof get washed into the gutter.
C. Leaves help gutters drain water.

UNIT 23

1. Sal liked to make ducks for people to put in their yards. She cut them out of wood. When someone wanted to buy one of the ducks, they told her what color to paint it. After three months Sal sold ten brown ducks, six yellow ducks, and four black ducks.

2. Juan had a small garden. Most of the time, he sold everything that he grew. People liked to buy his red, ripe tomatoes and big, yellow squash. This year he was going to do something new. One of his tomato plants had such large tomatoes he was sure he could win a prize for them. He took them to the fair. Juan was right. He won a prize for the biggest tomato.

3. A panda looks like a bear, but it is not really a bear. A panda is more like a raccoon. Bears eat meat, but pandas do not. Pandas eat only one kind of plant. They eat bamboo. This is why it is hard for pandas to live when bamboo plants are cut down.

4. Every map has a key. The key tells what the symbols on the map mean. A picture of a tent on a map might show where you can camp. The key would tell you what the tent means. A picture of a book might show where you can find a library. If you draw a map, you can decide what to put on it. You can decide what the symbols on your map will mean.

______ **1.** Which of these sentences is probably true?

A. Sal painted all the ducks as she made them.
B. Most people wanted brown ducks.
C. The unpainted ducks were the most popular.

______ **2.** Which of these sentences is probably true?

A. This year Juan did not sell all his tomatoes.
B. People liked the way Juan's garden looked.
C. Juan was a worker in someone else's garden.

______ **3.** Which of these sentences is probably true?

A. Pandas will eat grass, too.
B. Pandas cannot live without bamboo.
C. Bears like pandas because they eat bamboo.

______ **4.** Which of these sentences is probably true?

A. The mapmaker decides what should be in the key.
B. The map key tells which direction to go.
C. You don't need a key on a map.

UNIT 24

1. The whole family sat around the TV. Sy said to his dad, "I am hungry. Please fix me something to eat." His father said, "I will surprise you all." He went into the kitchen. The family could hear Dad as he worked in the kitchen. They heard pop, pop, pop. The house started to smell like a movie theater.

2. Long ago, men worked to cut trees and make them into logs. One day some men found gold where they were working. Soon people from towns nearby came to look for gold. They found more and more gold. Then people from all over the world came to look for gold. Hundreds of thousands of people came to look for gold so they could be rich.

3. A desert does not get much rain. There are no lakes or streams in the desert. Plants in a desert need to be able to hold water for a long time. A cactus plant keeps water in its stem and leaves. These plants have sharp thorns. These thorns stick animals who try to eat the leaves or stems.

4. At a track meet, you can see people jump, run, and throw. People run different kinds of races at a track meet. People run long and short races. They run races in which they jump over hurdles. At a track meet, people throw an iron ball as far as they can. This is called the shot put. People also use a pole to jump over a bar. Some people have jumped over a bar 21 feet above the ground.

______ **1.** Which of these sentences is probably true?

A. Dad was making popcorn for the family.
B. The toaster broke, and it made a popping sound.
C. Dad left and went to the movies by himself.

______ **2.** Which of these sentences is probably true?

A. Only people nearby came to find gold.
B. News of the gold spread fast.
C. The workers tried to hide the gold.

______ **3.** Which of these sentences is probably true?

A. Plants that need much water don't live in deserts.
B. Animals don't live in deserts.
C. Plants get water from lakes in the desert.

______ **4.** Which of these sentences is probably true?

A. Everyone does the same thing at a track meet.
B. People in track meets have different skills.
C. Only girls can be in track meets.

UNIT 25

1. The bell rang. The boys came into the room. Some had their shirttails sticking out of their pants. Each one had a bat or a ball. All had red faces. They were glad to get into their seats.The teacher said it was time to get back to work.

2. Tony got up early each morning. He dressed, and then he helped his mother cook breakfast. They cooked ham and eggs. Tony set the table. His mother always gave him an extra cinnamon bun for helping her.

3. Lisa tore the paper off the box. She could not wait to open it. There was a wonderful brown duck inside. She placed it next to her other gifts. She already had a book and a doll. Then she and her friends ran to the table. Her dad brought in the cake.

4. Bill had not seen Sam all week. He rode over to Sam's house. He walked up and rang the doorbell. Sam's dad came to the door. "Can Sam play?" asked Bill. Sam's father said, "No. He is still in bed with a cold."

_____ **1.** Which of these sentences is probably true?

A. The boys had just come in from playing.
B. The teacher yelled at the boys.
C. The boys had just finished math.

_____ **2.** Which of these sentences is probably true?

A. Tony loved to eat cinnamon buns.
B. Tony was the last person to get out of bed.
C. Tony helped his father.

_____ **3.** Which of these sentences is probably true?

A. Lisa had a nice birthday party.
B. Lisa didn't like to eat cake.
C. Lisa's mother brought in the cake.

_____ **4.** Which of these sentences is probably true?

A. Bill was not able to play.
B. Bill wanted to play football.
C. Sam had been sick for a few days.

Think and Apply

Getting to Know You

Read each story. Think about each person in the story. Then look at the words in the boxes below. If a word tells about that person, write **yes** in the box. If a word does not tell about the person, write **no**.

Story 1 Sara and Chiang went for a trail ride on their horses. They waved to other riders they saw on the trail. Chiang wanted to race. But Sara said the trail was too narrow. Chiang started to race anyway. He rode right into a low branch and fell off his horse. Sara made sure Chiang was not hurt. Then she rode on to catch his horse. Sara led the horse back to Chiang. Chiang got back on his horse. He and Sara rode back to the barn.

	friendly	careful	foolish
Sara			
Chiang			

Story 2 Kate went fishing. She caught a large fish. She ran to show the fish to her mom and dad. They told her what a good job she had done. That night Kate and her parents had a tasty fish dinner.

	happy	unlucky	proud
Kate			

What's Next?

Read the first two sentences in each item. Then decide what will happen next. Write your answer for each item on the line below the sentences. The first one is done for you.

1. Matt wets his toothbrush with water.
   Matt puts toothpaste on his toothbrush.
   Matt brushes his teeth.
2. The phone rings.
   Jill runs into the kitchen.
   ____
3. The seeds have been planted.
   The farmer waters the seeds.
   ____
4. Today is Megan's birthday.
   There's a gift sitting on the table.
   ____
5. It is a hot day.
   The tiger comes to a river.
   ____
6. The school day is over.
   The children get on the school bus.
   ____
7. Mom writes a list of things we need.
   Mom goes to the grocery store.
   ____

To check your answers, turn to page 62.

Why in the World?

Read each story. Then read the question. Write your answers on the lines below each question.

1. Marie listened to the weather report. Then she looked out the window. She ran outside and closed her car windows. She went back into her house. Marie checked all of those windows to be sure they were closed, too.
Why did Marie close all of her windows?

____

____

____

2. Andy fell off his bike. He got up and looked at his elbow. He parked his bike and went into his house. He washed his elbow in the bathroom sink. Then he patted it dry and put a bandage on it.
Why did Andy clean and bandage his elbow?

____

____

____

3. The dog walked by a hognose snake. It started to bark. The snake rolled over onto its back. The dog sniffed the snake. Then the dog walked away.
Why did the snake roll over onto its back?

____

____

____

To check your answers, turn to page 62.

Check Yourself

Unit 1 pp. 6-7	Unit 2 pp. 8-9	Unit 3 pp. 10-11	Unit 4 pp. 12-13	Unit 5 pp. 14-15	Unit 6 pp. 16-17	Unit 7 pp. 18-19	Unit 8 pp. 20-21
1. C	**1. A**	**1. A**	**1. A**	**1. A**	**1. A**	**1. A**	**1. C**
2. A	**2. B**	**2. A**	**2. A**	**2. B**	**2. B**	**2. A**	**2. C**
3. A	**3. B**	**3. A**	**3. A**	**3. A**	**3. A**	**3. C**	**3. B**
4. B	**4. A**	**4. B**	**4. B**	**4. C**	**4. A**	**4. C**	**4. C**

Unit 9 pp. 22-23	Unit 10 pp. 24-25	Unit 11 pp. 26-27	Unit 12 pp. 28-29	Unit 13 pp. 30-31	Unit 14 pp. 32-33	Unit 15 pp. 34-35	Unit 16 pp. 36-37
1. B	**1. B**	**1. A**	**1. A**	**1. B**	**1. B**	**1. C**	**1. A**
2. C	**2. A**	**2. A**	**2. A**	**2. A**	**2. A**	**2. B**	**2. B**
3. B	**3. A**	**3. B**	**3. B**	**3. A**	**3. B**	**3. B**	**3. B**
4. A	**4. C**	**4. C**	**4. A**	**4. C**	**4. A**	**4. C**	**4. A**

Unit 17 pp. 38-39	Unit 18 pp. 40-41	Unit 19 pp. 42-43	Unit 20 pp. 44-45	Unit 21 pp. 46-47	Unit 22 pp. 48-49	Unit 23 pp. 50-51	Unit 24 pp. 52-53	Unit 25 pp. 54-55
1. A	**1. C**	**1. A**	**1. A**	**1. A**	**1. C**	**1. B**	**1. A**	**1. A**
2. B	**2. C**	**2. A**	**2. A**	**2. B**	**2. A**	**2. A**	**2. B**	**2. A**
3. C	**3. A**	**3. C**	**3. A**	**3. A**	**3. B**	**3. B**	**3. A**	**3. A**
4. A	**4. A**	**4. C**	**4. A**	**4. B**	**4. B**	**4. A**	**4. B**	**4. C**

Practice Making Inferences, Page 4

2. A

Getting to Know You, Page 56

Story 1:

	friendly	careful	foolish
Sara	yes	yes	no
Chiang	yes	no	yes

Story 2:

	happy	unlucky	proud
Kate	yes	no	yes

What's Next? Page 57

2. Jill answers the phone.
3. The seeds grow into plants.
4. Megan opens the gift.
5. The tiger gets a drink of water or goes swimming.
6. The children ride home on the bus.
7. Mom buys the things on the list.

Why in the World? Page 58

1. Marie knew it was going to rain.
2. Andy hurt his elbow when he fell off his bike.
3. The snake played dead so the dog would leave it alone.